2 CORINTHIANS

THEOLOGY OF WORK PROJECT

2 CORINTHIANS

THE BIBLE AND YOUR WORK
Study Series

HENDRICKSON
PUBLISHERS

Theology of Work
The Bible and Your Work Study Series: 2 Corinthians

© 2015 by Hendrickson Publishers Marketing, LLC
P.O. Box 3473
Peabody, Massachusetts 01961-3473

ISBN 978-1-61970-686-6

William Messenger, Executive Editor, Theology of Work Project
Sean McDonough, Biblical Editor, Theology of Work Project
Patricia Anders, Editorial Director, Hendrickson Publishers

Contributors:
Valerie O'Connell, "2 Corinthians" Bible Study
Joel R. White, "2 Corinthians and Work" in the *Theology of Work Bible Commentary*

The Theology of Work Project is an independent, international organization dedicated to researching, writing, and distributing materials with a biblical perspective on work. The Project's primary mission is to produce resources covering every book of the Bible plus major topics in today's workplaces. Wherever possible, the Project collaborates with other faith-and-work organizations, churches, universities and seminaries to help equip people for meaningful, productive work of every kind.

Printed in the United States of America

First Printing—September 2015

Contents

The Theology of Work

Work is not only a human calling, but also a divine one. "In the beginning God created the heavens and the earth." God worked to create us and created us to work. "The LORD God took the man and put him in the garden of Eden to till it and keep it" (Gen. 2:15). God also created work to be good, even if it's hard to see in a fallen world. To this day, God calls us to work to support ourselves and to serve others (Eph. 4:28).

Work can accomplish many of God's purposes for our lives—the basic necessities of food and shelter, as well as a sense of fulfillment and joy. Our work can create ways to help people thrive; it can discover the depths of God's creation; and it can bring us into wonderful relationships with co-workers and those who benefit from our work (customers, clients, patients, and so forth).

Yet many people face drudgery, boredom, or exploitation at work. We have bad bosses, hostile relationships, and unfriendly work environments. Our work seems useless, unappreciated, faulty, frustrating. We don't get paid enough. We get stuck in dead-end jobs or laid off or fired. We fail. Our skills become obsolete. It's a struggle just to make ends meet. But how can this be if God created work to be good—and what can we do about it? God's answers for these questions must be somewhere in the Bible, but where?

The Theology of Work Project's mission has been to study what the Bible says about work and to develop resources to apply the Christian faith to our work. It turns out that every book of the Bible gives practical, relevant guidance that can help us do our jobs better, improve our relationships at work, support ourselves, serve others more effectively, and find meaning and value in our work. The Bible shows us how to live all of life—including work—in Christ. Only in Jesus can our work be transformed to become the blessing it was always meant to be.

To put it another way, if we are not following Christ during the 100,000 hours of our lives that we spend at work, are we really following Christ? Our lives are more than just one day a week at church. The fact is that God cares about our life *every day of the week*. But how do we become equipped to follow Jesus at work? In the same ways we become equipped for every aspect of life in Christ—listening to sermons, modeling our lives on others' examples, praying for God's guidance, and most of all by studying the Bible and putting it into practice.

This Theology of Work series contains a variety of books to help you apply the Scriptures and Christian faith to your work. This Bible study is one volume in the series The Bible and Your Work. It is intended for those who want to explore what the Bible says about work and how to apply it to their work in positive, practical ways. Although it can be used for individual study, Bible study is especially effective with a group of people committed to practicing what they read in Scripture. In this way, we gain from one another's perspectives and are encouraged to actually *do* what we read in Scripture. Because of the direct focus on work, The Bible and Your Work studies are especially suited for Bible studies *at* work or *with* other people in similar occupations. The following lessons are designed for thirty-minute lunch breaks, although they can be used in other formats as well.

Christians today recognize God's calling to us in and through our work—for ourselves and for those whom we serve. May God use this book to help you follow Christ in every sphere of life and work.

Will Messenger, Executive Editor
Theology of Work Project

Introduction to 2 Corinthians

The Apostle Paul wrote 2 Corinthians to real people in a real church, one that he had founded in Corinth, a coastal town thirty miles or so outside of Athens. His relationship with the church in this town—severely strained by "disputes without and fears within" (2 Cor. 7:5)—had recently improved. But problems such as false apostles preaching false messages remained and needed to be addressed.

This church, like the others Paul founded or served, was Paul's workplace. Although it might seem that a church is a very different kind of workplace than the companies, agencies, governments, families, schools, stores, and other places where most people work, most of the issues discussed in 2 Corinthians are common to all workplaces. Paul covers topics including transparency, joy, sincerity, reputation, service, humility, leadership, performance and accountability, reconciliation, working with nonbelievers, encouragement, generosity, timely fulfillment of obligations, and the proper use of wealth. Wherever you work, there is much you can learn from studying 2 Corinthians.

Second Corinthians offers us a unique glimpse into the heart and soul of this apostle. We see Paul at work modeling the attributes and importance of strong relationships as he contends for the integrity of the church. The first seven chapters of 2 Corinthians express Paul's joy and gratitude to both God and the Corinthians for the restoration of his relationship with them. In chapters 8 and 9 he turns to the topics of generosity and timely fulfillment of obligations, as he exhorts the Corinthians to fulfill their earlier promise to contribute to the relief of Christians in Jerusalem. The remaining chapters, 10 through 13, address the accusations and false teachings that were currently undermining this church.

Paul also found himself in the painful position of having to defend his reputation as well as his authority as an apostle. Although the attacks were deeply personal, the vigorous defense Paul makes is not. He offers his defense in order to uphold the integrity of the gospel of Jesus Christ. For then, as now, our actions and reputations as Christians reflect on our God to a fallen world. Again, as he works through the struggles in his workplace, Paul serves as a model and encouragement for all Christians in our myriad places of work.

Throughout this letter, Paul challenges us to trust God's strength in our weakness, as we honor the responsibility of carrying the knowledge of the glory of God in fragile jars of clay. This study is written for anyone who wants to learn how to be more effective in their work—and anyone who is willing to trust God for the ability to do so. We will find a practical model in Paul and his teachings in 2 Corinthians, all of which are rooted in the deep sufficiency of God's grace in our lives. This study welcomes you into a new relationship with your God and your co-workers.

Chapter 1

Relationships at Work

(2 Corinthians 1)

Lesson #1: God's Grace Builds Relationships

Second Corinthians begins with Paul's benediction, "Grace and peace to you from God our Father and the Lord Jesus Christ" (2 Cor.1:2). He then considers the deep relationship he has with the Corinthians: "As you share in our sufferings, so you also share in our consolation" (2 Cor. 1:7). Paul and the church at Corinth are so closely knit together that whatever happens to one is experienced as if it had happened to the other, a description that sounds almost like a marriage.

Given the strained relationship between Paul and the church that comes into view during the letter, this intimacy may be surprising. How could people who experience such disagreements, disappointments, and even anger at each other say, "Our hope for you is unshaken" (2 Cor. 1:7)? The answer is that good relationships do not arise from mutual agreement, but from mutual respect in the pursuit of a common goal. This aspect of relationships is a pivotal factor in our work.

We do not generally have the opportunity to choose our co-workers any more than the Corinthians chose Paul to be their apostle. Nor did Paul choose which Corinthians God would lead to faith. Our relationships at work are not based on mutual attraction, but on the need to work together to accomplish our common tasks and goals. Our work matters to God. And our relationships are among the most fundamental tools of our work. Whether our work is to plant churches, manufacture auto parts, or process insurance and government forms, the more difficult the circumstances the more important good relationships become.

How do we build good relationships at work? Paul makes it clear that we cannot achieve good relationships through skillful methods alone. What we need above all is God's grace. For this reason, praying for each other is the cornerstone of good relationships. "Join in helping us by prayers," Paul asks, and then speaks of "the blessing granted to us through the prayers of many" (2 Cor. 1:11).

The people we work with may not share our faith, but people almost always appreciate an authentic offer to pray for them, especially when great fear visits and tragedy strikes their lives.

 Food for Thought

How deeply do you invest in relationships with the people you work with every day? How well do you care for them? Do you ever ask the people in your workplace whether you can pray for them? How do you think that offer would be received? Would your management approve or be critical? Write down some specific needs or concerns of your co-workers, and then pray for them.

_____

_____

_____

_____

_____

_____

Recall the worst day you've had at work in the past month. What made it so bad? Now picture what the day might have been like had you prayed before you reacted. What difference might that prayer have made in that day's problems?

_____

_____

_____

_____

_____

_____

_____

Prayer

Father,

I ask that your grace be alive in my life. Help me to learn enough about my co-workers so I can pray for them specifically and care enough to pray for them daily.

Amen.

Lesson #2: Transparency Is Honesty in Action

As Paul moves into the body of his second letter to the Corinthians, he addresses the accusation of dishonesty. Though Paul's integrity has been questioned, he knows he has established a history of being transparent with them, one that should serve as a basis for their continued trust in him. He reminds them of this: "We have behaved in the world with frankness and godly sincerity" (2 Cor. 1:12). Having seen him in action, they know he says what he means without vacillation (2 Cor. 1:17–20).

Paul mentions behavior, frankness, and godly sincerity. Transparency is more than the absence of lies or even of simply being honest. It is openness, done with honesty, for the sake of a relationship rather than personal gain. Transparency is honesty in action—a powerful basis for building trust and relationships.

In today's workplace, communication is the vehicle for translating private honesty and values into productive transparency. From quick conversations in the hallway to a company-wide e-mail—with all kinds of meetings, texts, instant messages, and posts in between—the opportunities for communication have never been greater. And with those opportunities come risk, misunderstandings, overload, and dilution of messages. In this environment, transparency requires that we make a sustained effort to be consistently honest, open, and deeply sincere about the health of our relationships. The question is not how to avoid lying, but how to communicate so that others gain an accurate understanding of things.

Of course, being transparent doesn't mean that we reveal all the information we have. There is no need to overshare. At work there is also the issue of confidentiality. When it comes to transparency, the difference between enough and too much information frequently lies in careful consideration of our motives for sharing, and the good it will do for others. May we, like Paul be able to say to everyone in our workplace, "We refuse to practice cunning or to falsify God's word; but by the open statement of the truth we commend ourselves" (2 Cor. 4:2). "We have spoken frankly to you Corinthians; our heart is wide open to you" (2 Cor. 6:11).

 *Food for Thought*

When questions arise about his ministry, Paul can appeal to his earlier dealings with the Corinthians because he knows that he has always been honest with them. If your reputation were under attack at work, how would you defend it?

_____

_____

_____

_____

_____

_____

Have you ever mistakenly hit "reply all," sending an e-mail that becomes an embarrassment to you when it reaches its unintended audience? How would that experience have been different if you had been diligently practicing transparency as a discipline and a core value in your work life?

_____

_____

_____

_____

_____

_____

On a daily basis, we face the temptation to hide the truth in ways that are not direct lies—such as obscuring motivations to falsely gain the trust of a customer or a rival, making decisions in secret to avoid accountability, hiding factors others would object to, or pretending to support co-workers in their presence but speaking derisively behind their backs. Ask yourself: If your co-workers can't trust you, how can God?

Prayer

> *God,*
>
> *Please help me to be honest with myself, open to my co-workers, and transparent in all my dealings for the good of all and your honor.*
>
> *Amen.*

Lesson #3: Joy Is Working for Others

Joy is the next means of building relationships that Paul discusses. "I do not mean to imply that we lord it over your faith; rather we are workers with you for your joy, because you stand firm in the faith" (2 Cor. 1:24). Even though he was an apostle with God-given authority, Paul brought joy to others by the way he led them—not lording it over them, but working alongside them. This style helped make him an effective leader who inspired the people associated with him to become strong and reliable co-workers.

Paul's words echo what Jesus said to his disciples when they argued over which one of them was the greatest: "The kings of the Gentiles lord it over them; and those in authority over them are called benefactors. But not so with you; rather the greatest among you must become like the youngest, and the leader like one who serves" (Luke 22:25–26).

Paul maintains that the essence of Christian work is working alongside others to help them attain greater joy as they accomplish their purposes. Joy in this sense is not the brief feeling of happiness that comes with fun or unexpected good fortune; it is the deep delight of working in accordance with God's design. What would our workplaces look like if we tried to bring others joy through the way we treat them? This idea does not mean trying to make everyone happy all the time, but treating co-workers and clients as people of value and dignity, as Paul did. When we pay attention to others' needs at work, including the need to be respected and entrusted with meaningful work, we follow Paul's own example. When we set aside our privileges to joyfully serve others and work for their good with no expectation of return, we follow the example of Jesus.

 Food for Thought

How would your work be different if you strove for a deep sense of mutual satisfaction in your dealings with co-workers and clients? What would you need to change to make bringing joy to others a top goal at work?

_____

_____

_____

_____

_____

_____

Often we wish we had a job with higher pay, greater prestige, more power, fewer demands, fancier perks. But if joy was the reward you sought and you could choose your role, which would you choose? What can you do today to bring joy to someone in your workplace—or even to yourself?

_____

_____

_____

_____

_____

_____

_____

One aspect of joy is the deep delight of working in accordance with God's design. What factors are in your control at your workplace? Which are in accordance with God's design? Which need adjustment, and how?

_____

_____

_____

_____

_____

_____

_____

In workplaces that are stressful and unjust, it's harder to experience and facilitate joy. Write down a few examples of joy and stress coexisting in your workplace. Does this bring to mind any ways you can find (and bring) joy even in stressful situations?

_____

_____

_____

_____

_____

_____

_____

_____

Prayer

Jesus,

You put every right aside to come serve us. Help me to put the joyful good of others ahead of my own, so my workplace might be more productive and open to your light.

Amen.

Chapter 2

Relationships that Work

(2 Corinthians 2–3)

Lesson #1: Priority Demonstrates Value

Relationships matter to God and to our work. We see Paul placing a high priority on his relationship with those in Corinth when, starved for news of them—news he had expected to hear from Titus—Paul cuts short his work in Troas. As he puts it, "My mind could not rest because I did not find my brother Titus there" (2 Cor. 2:13). He simply cannot attend to his work, his very passion, because of the anguish he feels over his strained relationship with the Corinthian believers. So he leaves a positive beginning in a city of great strategic importance in the hope of finding Titus, and with him, news of the church at Corinth.

Because Paul finds significant value in his relationships with other believers, he cannot conduct business as usual while these relationships are in disrepair. We cannot say with absolute certainty that he was familiar with Jesus' teaching about leaving one's gift at the altar and being reconciled to one's brother (Matt. 5:23–24), but he clearly understood the principle. Paul is eager to see things patched up, and he invests a great deal of energy and prayer in pursuing that end.

Paul's first goal is to bring about this reconciliation, even if it causes a significant delay in his work schedule. He does not try to convince himself that he has a great opportunity for ministry that will not come around again. Repairing the rupture in his relationships takes precedence over his work goals.

We cannot always drop what we're doing at a moment's notice to attend to strained relationships. But in the spirit of Matthew 5:23–24, when we learn (or even suspect) that a relationship has been strained or broken in the course of our work, we do well to ask ourselves which is more pressing at the moment—the completion of the task, or the restoration of a relationship. One of the best ways we can build healthy relationships at work is to make doing so a high priority, and then put in the time and effort.

 Food for Thought

Imagine you have taken a stand against a project your co-worker proposed. Although you acted fairly, your co-worker is still angry and hurt. What responsibility, if any, do you have to make that person feel better? What can you do?

_____

_____

_____

_____

_____

_____

_____

_____

Now imagine the same situation with one twist: uninformed on the matter, you took the wrong stand. What can you do to make this situation better and repair the relationship?

_____

_____

_____

_____

_____

_____

_____

Good relationships at work can improve productivity and morale, and reduce costs associated with turnover and mistakes. Fostering good relationships is good business. What factors work for or against the development of good relationships in your workplace? Is there anything you can do to make a difference?

_____

_____

_____

_____

_____

_____

_____

Prayer

> *Dear God,*
>
> *I need your grace and power to place the same priority on my relationships at work that you do. Please show me ways in which I can make things better, especially when I am wrong or wronged.*
>
> *Amen.*

Lesson #2: Sincerity Demonstrates Our Intentions

Paul finds himself again facing persistent questions about his character. The Corinthians seem to have been offended that he did not initially accept financial support from their church. His response is that supporting himself was a matter of sincerity. Not that there would be anything wrong with his receiving financial support. But he chose to forgo that right in order to clearly demonstrate the sincerity of the message he brought to these people. Paul explains:

> For we are to God the pleasing aroma of Christ among those who are being saved and those who are perishing. To the one we are an aroma that brings death; to the other, an aroma that brings life. And who is equal to such a task? Unlike so many, we do not peddle the word of God for profit. On the contrary, in Christ we speak before God with sincerity, as those sent from God. (2 Cor. 2:15–17)

If transparency is honesty in action, then sincerity is the demonstration of our intentions. People want to see whether we handle money in accordance with our high principles or ditch our principles when there's money to be made. "Everyone has his price," the saying goes. Is there a price at which your integrity is for sale? Our sincerity, or authenticity, reflects directly on the word of God in our workplace. We can demonstrate—and reinforce—our sincerity by simple actions that have become exceptional in many work environments. Here are a few ways to do this:

- Give credit to others freely and often when they have earned it.
- Deliver your promises on time, even if no one else respects deadlines.
- If you've made a mistake, admit it and apologize.
- If you've wronged a co-worker publicly, then make amends publicly as well.
- Be honest about your strengths *and* your weaknesses.

The question is not whether we can justify ourselves, but whether those around us can recognize that our actions are consistent with our Christian beliefs. If they are, then we are the fragrance of the knowledge of our God (2 Cor. 2:14).

 Food for Thought

Paul's choice and reasoning remind us that motivation is not just a private matter, especially when it comes to money. The way we handle money shines like a laser pointer on the question of our sincerity as Christians. If your co-workers saw your expense reports, timesheets, and tax returns, what would they conclude about your values?

_____

_____

_____

_____

_____

Imagine that your company has a strict and limited pool of money for raises and bonuses this year. A dollar given to one person is one less dollar available for another. Does this knowledge impact how strongly you advocate for your bonus? What is your reasoning?

_____

_____

_____

_____

_____

_____

_____

No one likes a co-worker who is self-righteous and holier-than-thou. But we are truly called to a higher standard of integrity than what many others are willing to accept. How can you behave to higher standards and yet do so in a way that honors God and shows sincerity?

_____

_____

_____

_____

_____

_____

_____

Prayer

Lord,

Help me to work according to your high standards, yet not consider myself better than anyone else. Strengthen my love for you so I may be sincere and compelling in all my actions at work today.

Amen.

Lesson #3: Reputation Is Built On Results

Paul asks the Corinthians two rhetorical questions, both of which anticipate a negative answer: "Are we beginning to commend ourselves again? Or do we need, like some people, letters of recommendation to you or from you?" (2 Cor. 3:1). Such letters, typically brimming with praise, were common in the ancient world, and best taken with a grain of salt.

Paul had no need of such letters in any case. The Corinthian believers knew him intimately. The only letter of recommendation he required was their very existence as a church, as well as their individual conversions in response to his ministry. In fact, Paul states that his letter of commendation is from Christ himself: "You yourselves are our letter, written on our hearts, known and read by everyone. You show that you are a letter from Christ, the result of our ministry, written not with ink but with the Spirit of the living God, not on tablets of stone but on tablets of human hearts" (2 Cor. 3:2–3). They could see the fruit of Paul's labor in their own lives, which left no doubt that he was an apostle sent by God.

Further, Paul insists he is not claiming competence in his own strength: "Our competence is from God" (2 Cor. 3:5). He has established a reputation built on results, not on claims of excellence—and he credits God with it all.

Reputation—for better or worse—has a direct bearing on our effectiveness at work today. If our reputation is good, then we find that our way tends to be smooth as we undertake projects and do our work. If our reputation is bad, then we find obstacles in our path and an uphill climb to add or demonstrate value. Although mistakes are made, injustices do happen, and it's possible to develop an undeserved reputation for a while, we generally earn the reputations we have by the way we act over time. Our reputation is a type of crowd-sourced appraisal that impacts our productivity—in our workplace and as bearers of the word of our God.

 Food for Thought

To a great extent, your reputation is shaped by how others perceive your actions. What can you do to be perceived more accurately? If your assessment is that your reputation is currently poor, what could you do to improve it?

_____

_____

_____

_____

_____

_____

_____

Think about your perception of others' actions, and how your conversations and behavior in your workplace may contribute to co-workers' reputations. Whose reputation have you built up? Whose reputation may you have damaged? Should you change how you handle this, and if so, how?

_____

_____

_____

_____

_____

_____

_____

Socrates is reported to have said, "The way to gain a good reputation is to endeavor to be what you desire to appear." For instance, if you really want people to see you as dependable, make certain you meet deadlines and follow through on promises. If you want to be seen as generous, be sure to notice and meet the needs of your co-workers. What do you desire to be when no one is watching? How can you translate that desire into actionable goals at work?

_____

_____

_____

_____

_____

_____

_____

_____

Prayer

Father,

I am no longer my own—I was bought at a great cost by your son. Show me how to best build and use my reputation and influence in ways that benefit others and honor you.

Amen.

Chapter 3

The Softer Side of Strength

(2 Corinthians 4)

Lesson #1: Humility Enables Transparency

In chapter 4, Paul returns to the theme of transparency, empha-
sizing the importance of humility in maintaining transparency.
Why humility? If we are going to let everyone see the reality of
our life and work, we had better be prepared to be humbled.

Being transparent with people would be easy if we had nothing
to hide. Paul says,

> Therefore, since through God's mercy we have this ministry, we
> do not lose heart. Rather, we have renounced secret and shame-
> ful ways; we do not use deception, nor do we distort the word
> of God. On the contrary, by setting forth the truth plainly we
> commend ourselves to every man's conscience in the sight of God.
> (2 Cor. 4:1–2)

But what if you're not perfect? It's one thing to be transparent
when our actions are noble, but another when transparency requires that we remain open even when we have behaved badly.

The truth is that we are all susceptible to errors of intention and
execution. Paul says that we are, in effect, clay jars, alluding to the
typical household vessels of his day. Made of common clay, these
jars were easily breakable, as are our best intentions. Our frailty
is no surprise to God or even to Paul, who finishes the thought
saying, "But we have this treasure in jars of clay to show that this

all-surpassing power is from God and not from us" (2 Cor. 4:7). The message this gives is that if God can work through us, he can certainly work through our co-workers as well.

Paul's confidence is not in his own rightness or ability, but in the power of God. Although we would far prefer to cover up our failings, God trusts us to let others see our errors and inadequacies. This trust prevents us from succeeding under false pretenses. When we freely acknowledge—to ourselves and others—that the good things we accomplish are not a reflection on us but on our Lord, the next logical step is to be humble. This humility in turn gives us the courage to be wrong in front of others. It enables us to admit our mistakes and look to God to put us back on track again—all the while maintaining the transparency that builds trusting relationships.

 Food for Thought

Humility is not always held in high regard in competitive workplaces. This valuation is partly due to a misunderstanding that defines humility as weakness. If your co-workers were to understand humility as a choice that requires great strength of character, would it fare any better? How would your workplace view true humility if it appeared?

In your work relationships, does humility have a role in your workplace behavior?

_____

_____

_____

_____

_____

_____

_____

Jane worked hard on a high-value project and received a bonus and public recognition for her achievement. In an effort to be modest, she downplayed her accomplishment, saying she contributed very little. Her co-worker Sally accused her of false modesty and called Jane's comments an ungrateful insult to the people who sought to recognize her. If you have been in a situation similar to Jane's or to Sally's, how did you respond? Which approach do you think most honors God, and why?

_____

_____

_____

_____

_____

_____

_____

Prayer

Holy Spirit,

Please work in my heart to build a healthy and grateful humility that keeps me transparent and open in all of my relationships.

Amen.

Lesson #2: Weakness Is a Source of Strength

From a human point of view, our weakness is a constant challenge to our willingness to remain transparent. It is a challenge to our pride and our wish to be well regarded. However, in God's economy our weakness is actually a source of our abilities. Paul writes that, regardless of what befalls us as believers, our eventual resurrection with Jesus is a certainty:

> Though outwardly we are wasting away, yet inwardly we are being renewed day by day. For our light and momentary troubles are achieving for us an eternal glory that far outweighs them all. So we fix our eyes not on what is seen, but on what is unseen since what is seen is temporary, but what is unseen is eternal. (2 Cor. 4:16–18)

Enduring suffering is not an unfortunate side effect experienced in some circumstances; it is the means of bringing about accomplishment. Just as the power of Jesus' resurrection came about because of his crucifixion, so the apostles' fortitude in adversity brings forth the power of God that is at work in them. In our culture, no less than in Corinth, we try to project strength and invincibility in order to succeed at work. We try to convince people that we are stronger, smarter, and more competent than we really are. No wonder Paul's message of vulnerability sounds challenging to us. Later in the letter he becomes even more explicit about God's strength in our weakness, recalling a time when he had asked God for relief:

> But he said to me, "My grace is sufficient for you, for my power is made perfect in weakness." Therefore I will boast all the more gladly about my weaknesses, so that Christ's power may rest on me. That is why, for Christ's sake, I delight in weaknesses, in insults, in hardships, in persecutions, in difficulties. For when I am weak, then I am strong. (2 Cor. 12:9–10)

The weakness stands in contrast to the largeness of the task. It is inadequacy, not incompetency, that Paul is promoting. He is not content to do poor work, but even his best is not enough to accomplish all that God wants to do through him. Paul doesn't sugar-coat the results. His inadequacies lead to insults, hardships, persecutions, and other difficulties. Yet if we hold up under difficult circumstances without trying to conceal or deny them, then we have the opportunity to demonstrate to our co-workers that we have a source of power outside of ourselves—the very power that effected Jesus' resurrection from the dead.

 Food for Thought

We know that the sufferings Paul counted to be "light and momentary" include a litany of pain, danger, and punishment unlike anything most of us will ever experience. Is there a situation at work that has been distressing you? How can you view it as "light and momentary," an opportunity for God to act?

_____

_____

_____

_____

_____

_____

If we can do a task on our own, how do we know that God is at
work? Which is more important to you—being seen as highly
competent, or as a servant of God? More likely, we do best when
we do both. How do you combine God's gifts to you with his
strength in your weakness?

_____

_____

_____

_____

_____

_____

We all want to be seen as ultra-competent, but sometimes God
works through other people to enable us to excel. Think of a time
when you exceeded your own expectations at work. Did others
partner with you or assist you? How did they "help you shine"?
What gifts did they bring to the table?

_____

_____

_____

_____

_____

_____

Prayer

Father God,

I thank you that my usefulness to you is not dependent on my strengths. Teach me to value the weaknesses that serve as a chance to glorify you.

Amen.

Lesson #3: The Leader as Servant

Transparency, humility, and weakness would be unbearable if our purpose in life were to make something great of ourselves and to be widely recognized for that greatness. But it is service, not recognition, that forms the Christian's true purpose. Writing a classic biblical statement on the concept that has come to be known as "servant leadership," Paul states, "We do not proclaim ourselves; we proclaim Jesus Christ as Lord and ourselves as your slaves for Jesus' sake" (2 Cor. 4:5).

Paul, the foremost leader of the Christian movement beyond the confines of Palestine, calls himself the slave of the Corinthians "for Jesus' sake" (2 Cor. 4:5). The ultimate servant-leader was, of course, Jesus. "For you know the grace of our Lord Jesus Christ, that though he was rich, yet for your sake he became poor, so that you through his poverty might become rich" (2 Cor. 8:9).

This fundamentally Christian insight should inform our attitude in any leadership position. This insight does not mean that we refrain from exercising legitimate authority or that we lead timidly. It does not mean that we tolerate complacency or poor performance. Rather, it implies that we lead with excellence because the results further others' well-being, rather than because they advance our careers or make us successful. In fact, as Christian leaders, we are called to seek other people's well-being ahead of our own. As slaves, we are compelled to do so. Jesus himself pointed out that a slave is required to work all day in the fields, come in to serve dinner to the household, and only then eat and drink (Luke 17:7–10).

Leading others by serving will inevitably lead to sacrifice, and it may also include suffering. The world is too broken for us to imagine that serving others will bring us only fair rewards and joy. Paul suffered affliction, perplexity, and persecution nearly to the point of death (2 Cor. 4:8–12), and then proceeded to count these facts as "light and momentary." In no way does this view mean we will be less effective than other leaders. It does mean that we cannot take the easy way out of difficult situations.

It is clear that Christian leaders and managers are called to put aside the privilege of taking care of themselves first in order to take good care of others. Serving others is not optional. When Christian workers who are not in management positions take this approach to their work and colleagues, they are clearly servants who hope to hear someday, "Well done, good and faithful servant."

 Food for Thought

A manager must lead and manage others, make decisions, and promote, lay off, or even fire workers. How can a Christian manager reconcile these roles with the call to serve others?

_____

_____

_____

_____

_____

Imagine that you are the manager of a department in a struggling corporation. You and the manager of another department have each put forth proposals. Only one will move forward, leaving the other department to face layoffs. You know the other should win. What do you do?

_____

_____

_____

_____

_____

_____

_____

Imagine that you are a janitor in a grocery store. How can you act as a servant-leader in your workplace? Would it be easier or more challenging to do this if you were the general manager? Why?

_____

_____

_____

_____

_____

_____

Prayer

Jesus,

Keep me focused on your incredible, sacrificial servant's heart that I may joyfully serve the people you have placed around me at work today.

Amen.

Chapter 4

New Creations at Work
(2 Corinthians 5)

Lesson #1: Performance and Accountability

In 2 Corinthians 5, Paul reminds his readers that at the final judgment each person will be "recompensed according to what he has done in the body, whether good or evil" (2 Cor. 5:10). These words may seem unusual for those of us who associate Paul with the doctrine of grace—the belief that our salvation is entirely unmerited and not the result of our own works (Eph. 2:8–9). But when we analyze Paul's teaching in its entirety, we find it is in harmony with that of Jesus, James, and the Old Testament.

All of these authorities are in agreement that a faith that does not express itself in good works is no faith at all. What we do in the body cannot help but reflect what God's grace has done for us. What pleases the Lord can be described either as faith or, as here, works of righteousness made possible by God's grace. Faith and obedience are so closely intertwined that Paul actually has both in mind here. Paul's message is clear enough: our faith determines how we live, not just what we say we believe.

In workplace terms, our performance matters. Moreover, accountability is the workplace equivalent of our giving an account to the Lord Jesus for all that we have done and left undone. Performance and accountability are profoundly important to the

Christian life. We cannot spiritualize these concepts or dismiss them as secular concerns of no importance to God. God cares if we neglect our duties, don't show up for work, or go through the motions without genuine attention to our work. He also cares when we work with all our hearts as if for him and when we excel.

God holds us to a high standard of conduct. One day we will answer for the way we have treated our co-workers, bosses, employees, and customers, not to mention our family and friends. Our creativity will be recognized, and so will our poor workmanship. This requirement to perform well does not negate the doctrine of grace, but instead shows us that God intends his grace to transform our lives.

 Food for Thought

God's idea of good performance may be different from the one held by your manager. Clearly you should follow God if meeting your employer's performance expectations requires unethical behavior—such as misleading customers or undercutting a co-worker. Have you had any instances like this? If so, how did you respond?

Take a moment to consider the parallels and differences between performance and accountability in our Christian and work lives. For one thing, God will judge us fairly where earthly managers may not. On the other hand, God knows the intentions of our hearts, which are invisible to our employers. What do the similarities and differences teach us about our responsibilities?

_____

_____

_____

_____

_____

_____

_____

_____

Prayer

> *Heavenly Father,*

> *Teach me to live out my life of faith in faithful works.*

> *Amen.*

Lesson #2: New Creations and Old Work

If performance and accountability sound as if Paul is calling us to grit our teeth and try harder, then we are missing a big point of 2 Corinthians. Paul intends for us to see the world in a completely new way, so that our actions stem from grace and this new understanding, not from trying harder. Paul says,

> Therefore, if anyone is in Christ, the new creation has come: The old has gone, the new is here! All this is from God, who reconciled us to himself through Christ and gave us the ministry of reconciliation: that God was reconciling the world to himself in Christ, not counting people's sins against them. And he has committed to us the message of reconciliation. (2 Cor. 5:17–19)

As members of this new creation we are transformed to become new creations ourselves. When we become believers and followers of the Lord Jesus, we are changed from the inside out, made new.

The mention of "creation" immediately takes us back to Genesis 1–2, the story of God's creation of the world. Work was part of God's original good creation. From the beginning, God intended that men and women work together (Gen. 1:27; 2:18), in concert with God (Gen. 2:19), to "till the ground" (Gen. 2:15), to "give names" to the creatures of the earth, and to exercise "dominion" (Gen. 1:26) over the earth as God's stewards. Right from the start, God's intention for his creation included work as a central reality of existence. It was only when humans disobeyed God and marred the creation that work became cursed (Gen. 3:17–18) and humans no longer worked alongside God.

God brings the new creation into existence by sending his Son into the old creation to transform or "reconcile" it. In Christ, God was reconciling the world to himself. Not just one aspect of the world, but the whole world. And we are his ambassadors.

Food for Thought

Do you feel like a new creation, or do you feel like the "old you" with new values? If you have been a believer for years, is there still anything new for you from God in your work? What changes do see in yourself, your thoughts, and your hopes as a result of an internal transformation?

_____

_____

_____

_____

_____

_____

Does being a new creation make it more likely that you will act in obedience to Jesus, or simply more painful when you fail? Are you aware of your newness when you are in your workplace, or do the demands of your job tend to dampen the urgency of your faith?

_____

_____

_____

_____

_____

_____

You are God's creation. You are his work. When you see yourself as God's work does it change how you view yourself and your work? Does this view increase or lighten your need to perform?

_____

_____

_____

_____

_____

_____

_____

We bring this new creation into a work world that is fallen and under the curse. And we bring it in jars of clay whose weakness is neither a surprise to God nor an excuse for our failings. How do you think work today differs from work as God had originally planned it to be before the Fall?

_____

_____

_____

_____

_____

_____

Prayer

Lord,

Although your word tells me that I am a new creation, so often I feel like I'm stuck in bad old habits, especially when I fail you. Help me to believe your word above my experience and to increasingly work in the strength of your power.

Amen.

Lesson #3: Ambassadors of Reconciliation

Those of us who follow Christ, who are reconciled to God by Christ, are in turn appointed to carry on Christ's work of reconciliation (2 Cor. 5:18). Paul tells us that we are ambassadors of Christ sent into a world that is broken and in pain to call everyone back to God. "We are therefore Christ's ambassadors, as though God were making his appeal through us. We implore you on Christ's behalf: Be reconciled to God" (2 Cor. 5:20).

As agents charged with bringing reconciliation to all spheres of the world, we are active in reconciliation between people and God (evangelism and discipleship), between people and people (conflict resolution), and between people and their work (improved quality of life and care for God's creation). There are three essential elements of the work of reconciliation. As ambassadors, we must:

1. Understand accurately what has gone wrong among people, God, and the creation from God's point of view. Without that understanding, we cannot bring genuine reconciliation any more than an ambassador could effectively represent one country to another without knowing what's going on in both.

2. Love other people and work to benefit them without judging them. Paul tells the Corinthians that he no longer looks at people from a human point of view (2 Cor. 5:16), but as a person for whom "Christ died and was raised" (2 Cor. 5:15). If we condemn the people in our workplaces or even withdraw from daily activities, we are regarding people and work from a human point of view. As we love the people we work with and try to improve their lives, our workplaces, products, and services, we act as agents of Christ's reconciliation.

3. Remain in constant fellowship with Christ.

If we do these things, we will be in a position to bring Christ's power to reconcile the people, organizations, places, and things of the world so that they too can become parts of God's new creation. Reconciliation is not something we do in addition to our work, but something we do *through* our work. If our work serves people's needs and enacts our respect and care for the people we work with, it is inherently an act of reconciliation.

 Food for Thought

The notion of reconciliation includes the idea of reuniting two parties who have been separated. In what ways do you see the effects of separation between God and the people in your daily work life? Take a moment to think about specific people, processes, and departments in your work world—picture them reconciled to God and pray for them right now.

_____

_____

_____

_____

In addition to doing your work itself as service to Christ, you may have the opportunity to tell people about his work of reconciliation. Evangelism in the workplace can be a tricky subject. Are there respectful ways you can tell others about Christ's work of reconciliation in your workplace? If evangelism is precluded from your portfolio of actions, in what other ways can you serve as an ambassador of Christ in your workplace?

_____

_____

_____

_____

_____

_____

_____

_____

Prayer

> *Jesus,*
>
> *You reconciled me to your Father through your death. Strengthen my will and soften my heart to reconcile others through your life in me. I especially pray for the people I work with to reunite with you.*
>
> *Amen.*

Chapter 5

Yokes at Work

(2 Corinthians 6)

Lesson #1: The Unequal Yoke

Paul has vividly portrayed the importance of good relationships with the people at our work. In his first letter to the Corinthians he made it clear that we should associate with non-Christians (1 Cor. 5:9–10), and he offers some suggestions on how to do so in 1 Corinthians 10:25–33.

But there are limits to the Christians' working relationships with non-Christians. In 2 Corinthians 6:14–18, Paul takes up the question of close relationships with non-Christians. Paul tells the Corinthians, "Do not be mismatched with unbelievers," as the New Revised Standard Version puts it, or to translate the Greek term *heterozygountes* more literally, "Do not be unequally yoked with unbelievers." His words are reminiscent of Deuteronomy 22:10, which prohibits yoking an ox and donkey together while plowing.

When two animals are yoked together, they are physically joined together in such a way that they must both move in lockstep. If one turns left, the other also turns left, whether or not it consents. This work arrangement is different from animals grazing in a herd. Herd mates cooperate but still have the freedom to move separately and even to depart from the herd if they choose. If two animals—or, metaphorically, two people—are yoked, each is bound by whatever the other chooses to do. Two people are yoked if one person's choices or decisions compel the other person to follow the same choices. To be unequally yoked with unbelievers, then, is to be in a situation or relationship that binds you to the decisions and actions of people who have values and purposes incompatible with Jesus' values and purposes.

What, then, are the limits in working with nonbelievers? When Paul tells us not to be unequally yoked in working relationships, he is warning us not to get entangled in work situations that prevent us from doing the work Jesus wants us to do or that prevent us from working in Jesus' ways. "What partnership is there between righteousness and lawlessness?" Paul asks (2 Cor. 6:14). We are unequally yoked if the dictates of a work situation lead us to harm customers, deceive constituents, mislead employees, abuse co-workers, pollute the environment, or violate our duties as stewards of God's kingdom.

 Food for Thought

Why does it matter to God that you avoid a relationship that binds you to the actions of a nonbeliever who is mismatched to your values? Does working for a non-Christian organization mean you are unequally yoked? Does working for a Christian employer ensure that you are equally yoked? If not, explain.

_____

_____

_____

_____

_____

_____

_____

_____

Imagine that the only job you can get is one that will definitely put you in a position that challenges your values as a follower of Jesus. But you also have a pressing God-given responsibility to support your family. What do you do, and how do you decide?

_____

_____

_____

_____

_____

_____

_____

Prayer

God,

I ask that you give me the wisdom to accurately weigh my choices and partnerships at work and in all aspects of my life.

Amen.

Lesson #2: The Yoke of Jesus

Paul does not want us to be unequally yoked. So what would it mean to be equally yoked? Jesus has already given us the answer to that question. "Take my yoke upon you," he calls to those who follow him (Matt. 11:29a). Paul tells us not to be unequally yoked with nonbelievers because we are already yoked to Jesus.

One part of his yoke is around us, and the other is on Jesus' shoulders. Jesus determines the bearing, pace, and path of the team, and we submit to his leadership. Through his yoke, we feel his pull, guidance, and direction. By his yoke, he trains us to work effectively in his team.

Being yoked with Jesus not only pulls us away from sinful or unethical behavior, but it also leads us into Jesus's work to restore the world to God's vision and purposes in every sphere of life. Jesus tells us, "My yoke is easy, and my burden is light" (Matt. 11:29b). It is easy, not because the work is easy, but because the partnership is strong. We are called to do God's work—work that cannot be done without him.

 Food for Thought

A business partnership with an unbeliever would generally seem to be a form of yoking. If one partner signs a contract, spends money, buys or sells property—or even violates the law— the other partner is bound by that action or decision. Even if the believer trusts that the nonbelieving partner would not do anything unethical, is it possible that the nonbelieving partner would hinder the believer from doing all the good Christ desires? Joining an army, making a pledge of office, raising money for a nonprofit organization, or buying property jointly might have similar consequences. Have you been in a similar situation? If so, how did you deal with it?

_____

_____

_____

_____

_____

_____

_____

_____

A single commercial transaction—buying or selling an item be-tween two parties—would generally not seem to be a form of yoking. The parties agree in advance on a single item of business and then perform what they agreed to. Neither party is bound by anything the other party might do after the transaction. Teaching a class, writing, or being interviewed for a newspaper article, volunteering in a civic event, and babysitting a child are other examples similarly limited in scope and duration.

Buying stock is probably somewhere in between. As part owners in the corporation, stock owners are morally—though probably not legally—bound by the decisions of the directors, executives, and other employees, but only for as long as they own the stock. Likewise, getting a job, joining a faculty, raising money for a nonprofit organization or political campaign, and signing a contract all commit us to living with the consequences of others' choices, but not forever.

Prayer

Jesus,

Thank you for inviting me into partnership with you. Increase my desire and ability to know and follow your direction every step of my life.

Amen.

Lesson #3: Working with Nonbelievers

We must be careful not to turn Paul's words into an us-versus-them mentality—Christians against nonbelievers. Paul knew as well as anyone that believers fall far short of the values and purposes of God. The warning to avoid being unequally yoked also extends to Christians whose conduct would pull us away from following Jesus. Just as importantly, we need to receive God's grace every day so that being yoked with us doesn't cause someone else to be pulled away from their calling to work with Jesus, or to seek him in the first place.

Nor can we judge or condemn nonbelievers as inherently unethical, since Paul himself refused to do so. "For what have I to do with judging those outside? . . . God will judge those outside" (1 Cor. 5:12–13). We are called not to judge, but to discern whether our working relationships are leading us to work for the purposes of God according to the ways of Christ. Perhaps the best guidance is to ask ourselves the question Paul asks, "What does a believer share with an unbeliever?" (2 Cor. 6:15). If the answer is that we share similar values and goals with respect to the work we undertake together, then it may serve God's will to work closely with nonbelievers.

You can assess the opportunities and risks by exploring in advance the commitments entailed in any work relationship. Consider how your individual capabilities and limitations might reduce or exacerbate the risk of being pulled away from working as God intends. This approach means that the decision-making process and result may be different for each person. Considering our differing strengths and weaknesses, a free association for one person could be a binding yoke for another. A recent graduate, for example, might find it relatively easy to quit a job, compared to a CEO with a large investment and reputation at stake. Whatever our position, we have a responsibility to consider the ties that can arise in every workplace relationship, job, partnership, and transaction.

 Food for Thought

Getting a job in most organizations is probably not a form of yoking. But going so far into debt that you can't afford to quit your job probably is. If you have lost the freedom to resign if the organization begins to pull you toward ungodly activities, you have lost your ability to choose. What are the pairings in your life that help or hinder your work with Jesus?

_____

_____

_____

_____

_____

_____

_____

We think so often about the effect of others on us. This metaphor of the yoke also puts responsibility on us as Christians to be good partners at work. In what ways do your behavior, actions, and choices impact the productivity of the people in your organization? Are there people who would be pulled off God's course by working with you? Are there any ways you could improve in this area?

_____

_____

_____

_____

_____

_____

_____

_____

Prayer

> *Dear God,*
>
> *Please guide me to work that yokes me with Jesus in whatever sphere you call me to. Please help me to be mindful that my entanglements at work are consistent with your ways and that I may be a good influence as I work with others.*
>
> *Amen.*

Chapter 6

Building Relationships that Work

(2 Corinthians 7–8)

Lesson #1: The Gift of Encouragement

Immediately after admonishing the Corinthians, Paul praises them. "I often boast about you; I have great pride in you" (2 Cor. 7:4). It may come as a surprise to find Paul boasting so unapologetically about the church in Corinth. Many of us have been brought up to believe that pride is a sin (which it is when we forget that all we have is a gift from our God) and even that pride in someone else's accomplishments is questionable.

Further, we might wonder whether Paul's pride in the Corinthians is misplaced. This congregation was beset with many difficulties, many of which were self-inflicted. Paul directed some stinging rebukes to them in his letters, and he wears no rose-colored glasses when it comes to the Corinthians. But Paul is entirely unabashed by such concerns.

He does not shy away from giving praise where praise is due, and it seems that he is genuinely proud of the progress the believers in Corinth have made in spite of his tense relations with them. He notes that his pride in them is well deserved, not a cheap trick of flattery (2 Cor. 7:11–13). He repeats this point in 2 Corinthians 7:14 when he says, "Everything we said to you was true, so our boasting to Titus has proved true as well." Praise must be genuine, and the reasons for giving it sincere.

Praise that is specific, accurate, and timely encourages co-workers, employees, and others with whom we interact at work. Inflated or generalized praise is hollow and even manipulative in its insincerity. But words of genuine appreciation and gratitude for work well done are always appropriate. They are evidence of mutual respect, which is the foundation of true community, and they motivate everyone to continue their good work. We all look forward to hearing the Lord say, "Well done, good and faithful servant" (Matt. 25:21 NIV), so it makes sense to be on the lookout for ways to encourage the people we work with today. Encouragement is a gift to the giver, the receiver, and the workplace.

 Food for Thought

It's interesting how quickly bad news travels and how shy praise can be. Have you been encouraged at work by someone, and if so, what did she or he do to encourage you? What might have been different had that person not reached out? If you have not thanked that person, make a note to do so.

_____

_____

_____

_____

_____

_____

_____

Think about your work environment. What aspects of it are encouraging, and what parts tend to be discouraging? Is there someone at work who needs encouragement or help? Write down some ways you could come alongside them to help. Praise tends to be verbal, but encouragement can take many forms— some as simple as a smile.

_____

_____

_____

_____

_____

_____

_____

_____

Prayer

God,

Thank you for the many ways you encourage me in my walk with you at work and at home. I want to be an instrument of your care, so I ask that you show me ways I can encourage others.

Amen.

Lesson #2: The Gift of Generosity

Chapter 8 opens with Paul's version of a fundraising letter. Paul begins his appeal by pointing to the exemplary generosity of the churches in Macedonia—churches that were poor and under severe trial. He implies that he expects no less from the Corinthians.

Paul observes that the believers in Corinth who have excelled in faith, in speech, and in knowledge should also strive to abound in the grace or "gift" of generosity. The term "gift" has a double meaning here. It has the sense of "spiritual gift," referring to God's gifts of the Holy Spirit, which believers are always blessed to receive and exhibit. It also has the sense of "donation" or "present," referring to their gifts of money to the collection. The double meaning makes it doubly clear that generosity is an essential result of the Spirit's work in our lives.

Although money is easy to quantify, generosity is not. It is first of all a matter of the heart, not a calculation. Speaking of the Macedonians' incredible generosity, Paul says, "They gave themselves first of all to the Lord, and then by the will of God also to us" (2 Cor. 8:5). Nor is generosity a matter of money only. We can be generous in service, in praise, in empathy, in respect, in welcome. In the workplace, a generous spirit is the oil that makes things run smoothly on a number of levels. Employees who sense that their employers are generous will be more willing to make sacrifices for their organizations when it becomes necessary. Workers who are generous with their co-workers will create a ready source of help for themselves and a more joyful and satisfying experience for everyone.

Generosity is a gift that benefits the givers and those who receive. It is an act of grace that serves as a way to test the sincerity of your love (2 Cor. 8: 8) and, for the believer, it is not optional.

 *Food for Thought*

Employers can be generous by taking time to mentor workers, providing a workplace of beauty, offering opportunities for training and development, genuinely listening to someone with a problem or complaint, or visiting an employee's family member in the hospital. Co-workers can offer generosity by helping others do their work better, making sure no one is left out socially, sharing praise, apologizing for offenses, and simply learning the names of workers who might otherwise be invisible to us. What opportunities do you have to be generous in your workplace?

_____

_____

_____

_____

We see that generosity is a requirement. Does this requirement mean that we have to give at all times, to all people, whenever we have the opportunity and the means? Imagine you are a sales representative competing with another representative for a major account. That person learns you uncovered some information that will give you a big competitive advantage and asks you to share it. Although you have no legal responsibility to do so, do you do it? Write down a possible scenario or an actual experience.

_____

_____

_____

_____

_____

Generosity is a gift whether we are on the giving or receiving end of the act. Think of a time when generosity impacted your life. Did you see God's hand in it then, or only later? Do you think giving money is easier or more challenging than giving time, energy, and care?

_____

_____

_____

_____

_____

_____

_____

_____

Prayer

   Jesus,

   Let your generosity challenge me to have a generous heart with everyone I touch at work today.

                           Amen.

Lesson #3: Reliability Trumps Eloquence

Paul reminds the believers in Corinth that they had already signaled their intention to participate in the collection for the churches in Judea during the previous year. They seem, however, to have become sidetracked. Perhaps lingering doubts about Paul's ministry and the tensions that surfaced during his previous visit play a role here. In any case, their effort is flagging, and at the time of Paul's writing they have not yet gathered all the contributions from individual members, as he had previously instructed them to do (1 Cor. 16:1–3). Paul's advice is straightforward: "Finish what you started."

> Last year you were the first not only to give but also to have the desire to do so. Now finish the work, so that your eager willingness to do it may be matched by your completion of it, according to your means. For if the willingness is there, the gift is acceptable according to what one has, not according to what one does not have. (2 Cor. 8:10–12)

Paul's advice is as relevant now as it was then, especially in our work. What we start we should finish.

Obviously, there are many situations in which circumstances change or other priorities take precedence so that we have to adjust our commitments. This is why Paul adds, "according to your means." But often, as in the Corinthians' situation, the problem is merely one of dragging our feet. Paul reminds us of the need to carry through on our commitments, especially when other people are counting on us.

This advice may seem too simple to need mentioning in the word of God. Yet Christians sometimes underestimate how important reliability is as a matter of witness. If we do not fulfill ordinary commitments at work, how can our other words or actions possibly convince people that our Lord will fulfill his promise of a better life, let alone an eternal one? It is better to deliver a promised report, part, or raise on time than to deliver a lunchtime argument for the divinity of Christ. Reliability trumps eloquence.

 *Food for Thought*

In what ways is reliability like truthfulness? Is being unreliable like lying or stealing?

_____

_____

_____

_____

_____

_____

Reliability at work is part of your character, and it reflects on your ability to effectively serve as an ambassador of Christ. Think of your workplace. If your co-workers, clients, and management were to rank you on your reliability, how would you do? What would they say you do well, and what would they say you need to improve?

_____

_____

_____

_____

_____

_____

Prayer

God,

Thank you for your unfailing reliability in my life. I ask to grow in your grace and to become a person who is known for rock-solid reliability.

Amen.

Chapter 7

Giving in God's Economy
(2 Corinthians 8–9)

Lesson #1: Sharing God's Wealth

Paul reminds the Corinthians of the underlying principle behind the collection. "It is a question of a fair balance between your present abundance and their need" (2 Cor. 8:14). It is not that the Judean churches should experience relief to the detriment of the Gentile churches, but rather that there should be an appropriate balance between them. The Judean believers were in need, and the Corinthian church was experiencing a measure of prosperity. The time might come when the tables would be turned, in which case aid would flow in the other direction, "so that their abundance may be for your need" (2 Cor. 8:14).

The principle that the richer should give their wealth to the poorer to the degree that everyone's resources are in "balance" is challenging to modern notions of individual self-reliance. But in the context of God's economy, it makes sense. The logic of Paul calling Christians "slaves for Jesus' sake" (2 Cor. 5:4) concludes that 100 percent of our wages and our wealth belong directly to God. They are gifts and we are their stewards.

Paul's purpose is not to create a particular social system, but to ask those who have money whether they are truly ready to put it at God's service on behalf of the poor. "Show them the proof of your love and of our reason for boasting about you," he implores (2 Cor. 8:24).

There can be no question about the pressing urgency of poverty, and we should have no reluctance to balance our use of money with the needs of others around the world. Paul's forceful words show that those who enjoy abundance cannot be complacent when so many people in the world suffer poverty. Christians need to be on the forefront of developing not only generous but also effective means of bringing poverty to an end.

 Food for Thought

How does the principle of sharing wealth to alleviate poverty in the world apply to the workplace? Many organizations have programs designed to reach out to disadvantaged groups with training and employment. But on personal level, what can you do to alleviate the "poverty" of others at work?

_____

_____

_____

_____

_____

_____

_____

_____

If we really believe that all we have belongs to God, why do we ever struggle with giving? God does not need our gifts; we need to give them. How have you grown in your giving? Where could you give more?

_____

_____

_____

_____

_____

_____

_____

Are there other ways to respond generously to poverty, in addition to giving? Can there be generous investing? Generous saving? Generous spending?

_____

_____

_____

_____

_____

_____

_____

Prayer

Father,

I don't always understand how to apply your teachings to my work, but I want to. Teach me to have a generous outlook to others where I work.

Amen.

Lesson #2: God's Abundance

Paul urges and reassures his listeners,

> Remember this: Whoever sows sparingly will also reap sparingly, and whoever sows generously will also reap generously. Each of you should give what you have decided in your heart to give, not reluctantly or under compulsion, for God loves a cheerful giver. And God is able to bless you abundantly, so that in all things at all times, having all that you need, you will abound in every good work. (2 Cor. 9:6–11)

Paul is aware that he must address a very human concern in a world of limited resources and answer the unspoken question, "If I give as freely as Paul is urging me to give, will there be enough left to meet my own needs?"

Making use of an agricultural metaphor, Paul assures them that in God's economy things work differently. Giving is not like dividing the harvest, in which a fixed amount must be distributed among everyone who receives a share. It is like planting the seed, expecting that when harvest time comes, there will be a bounty for all. He has already alluded to a principle from the book of Proverbs (Prov. 11:24–25), noting that the "one who sows sparingly will also reap sparingly, and the one who sows bountifully will also reap bountifully." Stating that "God loves a cheerful giver," he offers reassurance to the generous and cheerful giver. God can and will cause all sorts of blessings to abound.

Paul, therefore, assures the Corinthians that their generosity will not come at the risk of future poverty. On the contrary, generosity is the route to prevent future deprivation. "God is able to provide you with every blessing in abundance, so that by always having enough of everything, you may share abundantly in every good work" (2 Cor. 9:8). This characteristic is especially applicable at work. Eventually we all need help from others in our workplaces. If we have been generous in helping our co-workers, we find that we have a network of people happy to help us in our time of need.

Although Paul is clearly speaking of material generosity and blessing, the assurance of God's provision does not translate into an expectation of getting rich. The "abundance" Paul speaks of means "having enough of everything," not getting rich. We need not fear that by helping others succeed at work we will compromise our own well-being. God has promised to give us all that we need.

Likewise, we can help others look good at work without fearing it will make us look lackluster by comparison. We can compete fairly in the marketplace. We can pray for, encourage, support, and even assist our rivals because we know that God, not our competitive advantage, is the source of our provision. God does not promise true believers a big house and an expensive car. But he does assure us that if we look to the needs of others, he will look after ours.

 *Food for Thought*

We know that God is able to provide us with every blessing in abundance, but we sometimes wonder if he will provide for us. Does giving challenge your faith or grow it? If so, in what ways?

_____

_____

_____

_____

_____

_____

_____

_____

In tough economic times, many people worry about their job security. In turn, that worry can cause us to tighten our grip on our wallets and our willingness to help others succeed at work. How do bad times impact your generosity?

_____

_____

_____

_____

_____

_____

_____

Prayer

> God,

> *Help me to grow my capacity to give in all ways as grate-
> ful worship and cheerful thanks.*

> *Amen.*

Lesson #3: You Can't Out-Give God

Speaking of their giving, Paul says,

> This service that you perform is not only supplying the needs of
> the Lord's people but is also overflowing in many expressions of
> thanks to God. Because of the service by which you have proved
> yourselves, others will praise God for the obedience that accom-
> panies your confession of the gospel of Christ, and for your
> generosity in sharing with them and with everyone else. And in
> their prayers for you their hearts will go out to you, because of
> the surpassing grace God has given you. Thanks be to God for
> his indescribable gift! (2 Cor. 9:12–15)

What is the "indescribable gift" that God has given? Jesus is
God's indescribable gift. "God made him who had no sin to be sin
for us, so that in him we might become the righteousness of God"
(2 Cor. 5:21). God's indescribable gift required the unimaginable
generosity of his Son: "For you know the grace of our Lord Jesus
Christ, that though he was rich, yet for your sake he became poor,
so that you through his poverty might become rich" (2 Cor. 8:9).

Although God will never compel us to give, we are called to receive his indescribable gift with generosity that is joyful and full
of thanks. We can never out-give God.

 *Food for Thought*

Although it is impossible to compare our very best giving to God's generosity, take a moment to think of how you could be generous at work. How can you use your knowledge, time, influence, ideas, information, and faith to help others succeed? Has it ever occurred to you to give one of your ideas to a struggling co-worker to help kick-start a recovery? Could you let a well-qualified colleague know about an internal opportunity you might both want? Can you let your manager once again take credit for work you did without feeling resentment? How about mentoring someone? Get creative. What can you do?

_____

_____

_____

_____

_____

Imagine you could receive one act of generosity in your workplace. What would you choose? Now try to find a way you can most closely approximate that gift and give it to another person. Which person is about to receive what blessing today? Let this act feel like worship.

_____

_____

_____

_____

_____

Prayer

God,

Thank you for your indescribable gift of Jesus Christ. I ask that you open my eyes and my heart to give generously for the betterment of others. May this cheerful giving reflect the love and the hope of Jesus to my co-workers.

Amen.

Chapter 8

Grace at Work

(2 Corinthians 10–13)

Lesson #1: Assessment without Judgment

Performance assessments are a regular feature of today's workplace. It can be stressful for the person assessing the performance, and a little unnerving to those being assessed. As Christians, we may struggle with the task, whichever end of the assessment we are on. We are repeatedly told not to judge others, nowhere more simply than in Matthew 7:1 when Jesus says, "Do not judge, or you too will be judged." Defending himself in the face of attacks by a few people he facetiously calls "super-apostles" (2 Cor. 11:5), Paul offers insights that can be applied to the performance assessment process.

The false super-apostles had been criticizing Paul for not measuring up to them in terms of eloquence, personal charisma, and evidence of signs and wonders. Naturally, the standards they chose were nothing more than descriptions of their own talents and ministries. Refusing to be baited by their self-serving pretensions, Paul points out what an absurd game they were playing. "When they measure themselves by themselves and compare themselves with themselves, they are not wise" (2 Cor. 10:12).

But Paul is not timid about exerting authority over his assigned areas of responsibility. "We, however, will not boast beyond proper limits, but will confine our boasting to the sphere of service God himself has assigned to us, a sphere that also includes you" (2 Cor. 10:13). He says that he will not only protect but also punish as needed: "We demolish arguments and every pretension that sets itself up against the knowledge of God, and we take captive every thought to make it obedient to Christ. And we will be ready to punish every act of disobedience, once your obedience is complete" (2 Cor. 10:5–6).

When we have a responsibility to make fair assessments of performance, opportunities, outcomes, and the people involved for the good of the organization, we have a godly responsibility to make those calls. When we have a responsibility to have our performance assessed by others, we must be ready to accept fair criticism. Either way, we must do it fairly, according to just standards, and within the sphere of our role. The fact that there may be negative consequences for those we assess or for ourselves is a painful part of doing our jobs well.

 Food for Thought

Problems can arise when the standards by which we measure ourselves or others are biased and self-serving. In some organizations—typically those only loosely accountable to their owners and customers—a small circle of intimates may gain the ability to rate the performance of others primarily based on whether it falls in line with the insiders' self-interests. As Christians we measure success by God's assessment rather than by promotion, pay, or even continued employment. If you were the beneficiary of a slanted system, would you accept it to your benefit or attempt to reform it to your possible detriment? Would it make a difference? In what way? Have you been in such a system? What did you do?

_____

_____

_____

_____

_____

_____

How do you separate business assessments and decisions from the judgmental stance the Bible condemns? Do you find the line between the two to be blurred at times? How could transparency and prayer beforehand be beneficial?

_____

_____

_____

_____

_____

_____

_____

Prayer

Jesus,

Help me to keep my business assessments free of self-interest and a judgmental attitude.

Amen.

Lesson #2: The Sufficiency of God's Grace

Paul's words are as challenging to us today as they were to the Corinthians of his day. Here are some of his main points:

- Serving others, even to the point of suffering, is the way to be effective in God's economy, just as Jesus himself effected our salvation by his death on the cross and resurrection.

- While falling far short of Jesus' divine perfection, Paul is willing to be transparent and humble, to be an example of how God's strength overcomes human weakness. Because of his openness, Paul is credible when he claims that he is working according to God's purposes.

- Paul calls us to work alongside others to help them attain greater joy as they accomplish their purposes—the deep delight of working in accordance with God's design. He tells us that we should put this serving of others ahead of our own interests.

- We are called to give high priority to being reliable and sincere in our work relationships, giving encouragement and help generously in the knowledge that we can't out-give God.

- Generosity is not optional for a Christian. Our resources are all gifts from God, and he is free to require our time, talent, and money in the service of his purposes.

- We should make judgment-free decisions and assessments.

- At work, as in life, we are to be yoked with Jesus—not unequally in ways that will pull us or others away from God's best.

- We have the high calling and immense privilege of being ambassadors for Christ, charged with the task of reconciling the world to God.

We, like Paul, may ask, "Who is sufficient for this task?" Paul passes on to us the words he received from the Lord Jesus himself, "My grace is sufficient for you, for power is made perfect in weakness" (2 Cor. 12:9). God's grace was sufficient then. It is sufficient now. And it always will be.

 Food for Thought

In what areas of your life or work are you most aware of relying on the grace of God? In which areas do you find it most difficult to trust in God's sufficiency? Why?

_____

_____

_____

_____

It is likely that we more often feel like a jar of clay than an ambassador of the living God. While this is normal, it is not humble. God tells us that we are both and that his grace is sufficient for us. To behave otherwise is not humility but a lack of faith or even disobedience. How can you hold the sufficiency of God's grace as a central motivating factor in your job?

_____

_____

_____

_____

Paul says in 2 Corinthians 6:1, "As God's co-workers we urge you not to receive God's grace in vain." He is speaking about our effectiveness as co-workers with God, not about our salvation. How is it possible to receive God's grace "in vain"? In what ways are you God's co-worker at work?

_____

_____

_____

_____

_____

_____

_____

_____

Prayer

Father God,

Thank you for the indescribable gift of your son Jesus. Help me to make your grace real in my life and the lives of everyone I know.

Amen.

Lesson #3: Last Thoughts

The unique circumstances that led Paul to write 2 Corinthians resulted in a letter with many important lessons for work, workers, and workplaces. Paul repeatedly stresses the importance of transparency and integrity. He urges his readers to invest in good and joyful relationships at work and to vigorously pursue reconciliation when relationships are broken or challenged.

He measures godly work in terms of service, leadership, humility, generosity, and the reputations we earn through our actions. Arguing that performance, accountability, and the timely fulfillment of obligations are essential duties of Christians at work, he gives us guidance we can use in judgment-free decision-making at work. The opportunities, challenges, and responsibilities of working with nonbelievers point us as always to Jesus and his yoke.

A good place to end this study is where Paul began in 2 Corinthians 1:3–4.

> Praise be to the God and Father of our Lord Jesus Christ, the Father of compassion and the God of all comfort, who comforts us in all our troubles, so that we can comfort those in any trouble with the comfort we ourselves receive from God.

Whether giving comfort in sorrow, abundance in giving, joy in suffering, plenty in little, when we give freely we are giving from what God has first given to us. Paul assures us that in all of our giving—financial, professional, or personal—we increase rather than decrease our own security, because we come to depend on God's grace, power, and sufficiency.

 *Food for Thought*

Take a moment to reflect on the topics raised by Paul in 2 Corinthians. Were there topics or insights that surprised you or challenged you to look at old behaviors in new ways? Have you learned anything that can help you more effectively and joyfully serve others in your work day?

_____

_____

_____

_____

_____

_____

Of all the things that one person can give another—time, money, opportunity, friendship, a second chance, praise, recognition, advice, respect—what do you most wish you could receive? Is there anyone you can offer that to today?

_____

_____

_____

_____

_____

_____

Would it surprise you to know that there are people who have been praying for you as you worked through this material? Write down the names of one or two specific people you work with—maybe one you really like and another you'd like to mentor or encourage—and commit to praying for their success at work and for the opportunity to help them.

_____

_____

_____

_____

Prayer

Holy Spirit,

I ask that you come alongside me, bringing to mind the truth that the Father wants me to understand. Help me to put into heartfelt action all that you show me, that I may be a living thank you to my God.

Amen.

Wisdom for Using This Study in the Workplace

Community within the workplace is a good thing and a Christian community within the workplace is even better. Sensitivity is needed, however, when we get together in the workplace (even a Christian workplace) to enjoy fellowship time together, learn what the Bible has to say about our work, and encourage one another in Jesus' name. When you meet at your place of employment, here are some guidelines to keep in mind:

- *Be sensitive to your surroundings.* Know your company policy about having such a group on company property. Make sure not to give the impression that this is a secret or exclusive group.

- *Be sensitive to time constraints.* Don't go over your allotted time. Don't be late to work! Make sure you are a good witness to the others (especially non-Christians) in your workplace by being fully committed to your work during working hours and doing all your work with excellence.

- *Be sensitive to the shy or silent members of your group.* Encourage everyone in the group and give them a chance to talk.

- *Be sensitive to the others by being prepared.* Read the Bible study material and Scripture passages and think about your answers to the questions ahead of time.

These Bible studies are based on the Theology of Work biblical commentary. Besides reading the commentary, please visit the Theology of Work website (www.theologyofwork.org) for videos, interviews, and other material on the Bible and your work.

Leader's Guide

Living Word. It is always exciting to start a new group and study. The possibilities of growth and relationship are limitless when we engage with one another and with God's word. Always remember that God's word is "alive and active, sharper than any double-edged sword" (Heb. 4:12) and when you study his word, it should change you.

A Way Has Been Made. Please know you and each person joining your study have been prayed for by people you will probably never meet but who share your faith. And remember that "the Lord himself goes before you and will be with you; he will never leave you nor forsake you. Do not be afraid; do not be discouraged" (Deut. 31:8). As a leader, you need to know that truth. Remind yourself of it throughout this study.

Pray. It is always a good idea to pray for your study and those involved weeks before you even begin. It is recommended to pray for yourself as leader, your group members, and the time you are about to spend together. It's no small thing you are about to start and the more you prepare in the Spirit, the better. Apart from Jesus, we can do nothing (John 14:5). Remain in him and "you will bear much fruit" (John 15:5). It's also a good idea to have trusted friends pray and intercede for you and your group as you work through the study.

Spiritual Battle. Like it or not, the Bible teaches that we are in the middle of a spiritual battle. The enemy would like nothing more than for this study to be ineffective. It would be part of his scheme to have group members not show up or engage in any discussion. His victory would be that your group just passes time together going through the motions of just another Bible study. You, as a leader, are a threat to the enemy as it is your desire to lead people down the path of righteousness (as taught in Proverbs). Read Ephesians 6:10–20 and put your armor on.

Scripture. Prepare before your study by reading the selected Scripture verses ahead of time.

Chapters. Each chapter contains approximately three lessons. As you work through the lessons, keep in mind the particular chapter theme in connection with the lessons. These lessons are designed so that you can go through them in thirty minutes each.

Lessons. Each lesson has teaching points with their own discussion questions. This format should keep the participants engaged with the text and one another.

Food for Thought. The questions at the end of the teaching points are there to create discussion and deepen the connection between each person and the content being addressed. You know the people in your group and should feel free to come up with your own questions or adapt the ones provided to best meet the needs of your group. Again, this would require some preparation beforehand.

Opening and Closing Prayers. Sometimes prayer prompts are given before and usually after each lesson. These are just suggestions. You know your group and the needs present, so please feel free to pray accordingly.

Bible Commentary. The Theology of Work series contains a variety of books to help you apply the Scriptures and Christian faith to your work. This Bible study is based on the *Theology of Work Bible Commentary*, examining what the Bible says about work. This commentary is intended to assist those with theological training or interest to conduct in-depth research into passages or books of Scripture.

Video Clips. The Theology of Work website (www.theologyofwork .org) provides good video footage of people from the marketplace highlighting the teaching from all the books of the Bible. It would be great to incorporate some of these videos into your teaching time.

Enjoy Your Study! Remember that God's word does not return void—ever. It produces fruit and succeeds in whatever way God has intended it to succeed.

> "So shall my word be that goes out from my mouth;
>   it shall not return to me empty,
>   but it shall accomplish that which I purpose,
>   and shall succeed in the thing for which I sent it." (Isa. 55:11)

"This commentary was written exactly for those of us who aim to integrate our faith and work on a daily basis and is an excellent reminder that God hasn't called the world to go to the church, but has called the Church to go to the world."

BONNIE WURZBACHER

FORMER SENIOR VICE PRESIDENT, THE COCA-COLA COMPANY

Explore what the Bible has to say about work, book by book.

THE BIBLE AND YOUR WORK
Study Series